The Queen's Spy

Written by Sally Prue

Illustrated by Alan Marks

Published by Pearson Education Limited, Edinburgh Gate, Harlow, Essex, CM20 2JE
Registered company number: 872828

www.pearsonschools.co.uk

Designed by Bigtop
Original illustrations © Pearson Education Limited 2012
Illustrated by Alan Marks

First published 2012

21
10 9

British Library Cataloguing in Publication Data
A catalogue record for this book is available from the British Library

ISBN 978 0 435 07620 7

Acknowledgements
We would like to thank the children and teachers of Bangor Central Integrated Primary School, NI; Bishop Henderson C of E Primary School, Somerset; Brookside Community Primary School, Somerset; Cheddington Combined School, Buckinghamshire; Cofton Primary School, Birmingham; Dair House Independent School, Buckinghamshire; Deal Parochial School, Kent; Holy Trinity Catholic Primary School, Chipping Norton; Lawthorn Primary School, North Ayrshire; Newbold Riverside Primary School, Rugby and Windmill Primary School, Oxford for their invaluable help in the development and trialling of the Bug Club resources.

Every effort has been made to contact copyright holders of material reproduced in this book. Any omissions will be rectified in subsequent printings if notice is given to the publisher.

Contents

Chapter 1

Edward struggled wildly, but the man holding him was immensely strong and he never had a chance. In a few moments Edward's arms were pinned to his sides and a hand was pressed across his mouth.

He tried to bite, but the hand only clamped itself even more tightly round his face.

"Steady, lad, steady," said a low voice in his ear. "You don't want to be smothered, now, do you?"

Edward didn't. He stopped struggling and blinked wistfully at the evening sunshine that was streaming in through the doorway to the barn.

He'd come out to the barn to get some firewood, and someone had stepped out of the darkness behind him and grabbed him before he could even scream.

There was a beard tickling the back of Edward's neck.

"Now, my bonny lad," said the voice, hoarsely. "You have an honest face. You're no traitor, I'll be bound."

Edward managed to shake his head a little. Of course he wasn't a traitor. He was only twelve years old, and still at school.

The man spoke again.

"Your father owns this house?"

Edward nodded. The man holding him stank of sweat and ditches. He must be some filthy **vagrant** who'd been sheltering in the barn. There were more and more of them about lately, wandering around the country begging and stealing. Things had got so bad that even the group of travelling **minstrels** who used to visit the town had been banned.

"A respectable man, then, your father must be," said the voice. "I hope you take after him."

Of course Father was respectable. He was a glove maker, and Edward was looking forward to leaving school and starting to learn the trade. Edward nodded again.

"Very well," said the voice. "Then listen. I am a servant of Sir Robert Cecil. So you must keep quiet, understand?"

The hand across Edward's mouth loosened a little and Edward took in a huge breath. His mind was reeling with astonishment. *Sir Robert Cecil?* But Sir Robert Cecil was one of Queen Elizabeth's chief men!

"Good lad," said the voice, and let him go.

Edward took a quick few steps away and turned round. The man who had grabbed him had a huge pot-belly, a great untidy beard, and a very dirty **jerkin** torn in several places.

But surely a great man like Sir Robert Cecil, who was an advisor to the Queen herself, wouldn't have such a man anywhere near him?

"I see what you are thinking," said the man. "It's true, I'd not cut much of a figure at Court just now. Indeed," he went on, ruefully, "I think I would have to bathe in rosewater for a week before I was fit to enter the presence of the Queen again."

Edward's jaw dropped in awe.

"You've seen the *Queen*?"

"Hush!"

The man looked round hastily.

"Not so loud, young master. There are traitors about."

Edward felt as if he'd fallen out of a tree: things kept spinning dizzily past him before he had a chance to catch hold of them. Sir Robert Cecil? The Queen?

"Traitors?" he echoed, weakly.

The man took his elbow and leaned close to whisper. His teeth were black, but then lots of people at Court had black teeth because they ate so much sugar.

"You know, lad, that England has many enemies?"

"You mean like the Spaniards, and the Catholics?"

"That's right. But do you know that Sir Robert Cecil is master of all the Queen's spies?"

Edward blinked. He hadn't known that.

"We go everywhere," went on the man, still whispering. "Behind every hedge, under every window, in the shadow of every wall, listening out for plots and traitors."

Edward's eyes widened.

"And that's why you're here?"

The man tapped the side of his nose.

"I cannot tell you exactly why I am here," he said. "But I need your help, lad, if I am to foil a dreadful plot."

"Really? Me?" said Edward, his heart beating fast with excitement. "But what must I do?"

The man looked at him with bright blue eyes.

"The first thing I need is your secrecy," he said.

"I won't tell anyone!" said Edward, breathlessly.

The man nodded. "Good lad. Good lad. I can see I can count on you."

"Oh yes," said Edward. "At least ... if there's anything I *can* do, I'll help."

The man leaned close to Edward again.

"Well, then, how about some supper," he suggested. "Oh, and a nice soft blanket, too."

And he smiled a wide black smile.

The blanket was easy: there were several folded away for the winter in the great chest. Quite a lot of moth-repelling herbs fell to the floor as Edward pulled one out, but he kicked the sprigs under the chest out of sight.

Supper was harder, but Edward did his best. He cut two onions from their string in the kitchen (the man would have to eat them raw, but they couldn't make him smell any worse than he already did). Luckily it had been a bread-baking day, so Edward took a loaf and rearranged the others so you couldn't tell there was one missing.

He got back to the barn without seeing anyone.

The man peered at the food Edward held out to him.

"No **ale**?" he said, blankly; and then, more shocked still: "And no meat?"

Edward was trying to work out how to start explaining when a voice behind him spoke.

"No respectable man eats meat on a Friday!"

Edward whipped round.

His sister Bridget was standing silhouetted in the doorway, her egg basket on her hip. Bridget was Edward's twin, and she was actually a few moments younger than Edward, but you'd never have thought it from the way she was always bossing him about.

Bridget stepped into the barn and snatched the loaf and the onions from Edward's hands.

"I wondered why you were skulking about in the kitchen," she told him. "What on earth do you think you're doing giving good food to this great lump? Look at him – a rump-fed vagrant who should be working!"

"But Bridget," began Edward, full of horror. "You don't understand! This is –"

She snorted.

"I understand well enough. And I'm calling the constable!"

The intruder was fat, but he could move amazingly fast. Before Bridget could turn round he was somehow between her and the doorway, and he was bowing to her with surprising grace.

"Gentle mistress," he said. "I beseech you –"

"And you needn't try and get round *me*," said Bridget, firmly. "We don't want your sort round here, robbing and drinking and causing trouble. Be off with you, or you'll find yourself being whipped through the streets!"

Edward was quite faint with alarm. To think

of such things being said to someone who worked for Sir Robert Cecil!

"Bridget," he said urgently. "Bridget, this gentleman –"

"*Gentleman?*" echoed Bridget, rolling her eyes. "Edward, you must be crazed. Our old pig is as much a gentleman as this lout!"

Edward nearly died of horror.

"He's been sent by Sir Robert Cecil!" he whispered, urgently.

Bridget sighed.

"You thick-headed loon," she said to Edward, pityingly. "No wonder Ralph Thatcham keeps whipping you. You're so stupid sometimes I'm surprised you know which end of your **quill** to dip into the ink. This is just a –"

"Ralph Thatcham?" said the man, quickly. "You know Ralph Thatcham?"

Bridget was such a show-off she couldn't resist answering him.

"He's Edward's schoolmaster," she told him, "and, frankly, I don't know which of them I feel more sorry for."

The man drew himself up to his full height, and suddenly there was something almost noble about him, despite his torn jerkin.

"Then at last I have found the villain!" he said. "And soon, with heaven's help, the Queen shall be safe from his evil plot!"

"Master Thatcham's plot?" breathed Edward, his eyes bulging in wonder and utter amazement.

Bridget turned her eyes to the dark roof of the barn.

"Huh," she said.

Chapter 2

Edward stared at the filthy pot-bellied man, hardly believing his ears.

"Master Thatcham?" he said. "Master Thatcham is a *traitor*?"

The man nodded curtly.

"Of the deepest and most deadly kind," he said.

Bridget snorted.

"Ralph Thatcham is nothing but a droning schoolmaster," she told them, "and given the amount he's taught Edward, he's not even any good at that. He's hardly got the sense to put his **hose** on the right way round, let alone think up some plot!"

The man nodded again.

"Witness the man's cunning," he said. "You see, Mistress Bridget, in the world of spies and traitors, nothing is what it seems. And that includes me, of course. I am Nat Cobbley, secret servant of Sir Robert Cecil, and I command you both to help me in the name of the Queen!"

It all made perfect sense to Edward.

"I always knew there was something wrong with Master Thatcham," he said. "I mean, why should anyone like him become a schoolmaster?"

"Because the pay is terrible, the schoolhouse is falling down, and the schoolmaster isn't even allowed to get married," said Bridget, crisply. "The **aldermen** have to give any clay-brained measle the job or there'd be no one to do it."

"Yes, but why would even *Master Thatcham* want to do it?" persisted Edward. "He really *hates* boys. He whips us all the time for nothing. Sometimes in the winter he whips us just to get himself warm!"

"A dastardly fellow indeed," agreed Cobbley. Bridget just gave Edward a withering look.

"You've never heard of a schoolmaster who *didn't* whip his pupils, have you?" she pointed out. "Anyway, I thought you said that he whipped you today because you didn't know your lesson?"

Edward flushed.

"Well, perhaps I did get a bit confused," he admitted. "Not that I'm going to need to know Latin if I'm going to be a glove maker like Father. Anyway, there was no need –"

"Enough!" Nat Cobbley was holding up his hand in a commanding gesture. "You need have no more fears, Master Edward, because if my investigation goes to plan, then Master Thatcham will not be your schoolmaster any more."

Edward gasped.

"Really?"

Bridget tutted.

"Of course not really," she said. "This fool's just an ale-headed vagrant."

Edward took no notice. He couldn't bear to let go of this wonderful hope. As things were, he woke up every morning feeling sick with dread. The thought of being free of Master Thatcham ...

Cobbley looked very serious.

"Mistress Bridget," he said, "I pray you. Think what might happen if you fail to help me capture a traitor."

That was an even more alarming thought. Edward clutched her arm. "They'd hang you!" he said. "Perhaps they'd **draw and quarter** you, too!"

Even Bridget hesitated at that.

"It can't do any harm to keep Master Cobbley safe for tonight, can it?" urged Edward.

But before Bridget could reply there was a shout from the house that made them both jump.

"Edward! Where are you, you idle boy? I sent you out for that wood half an hour ago. When I get hold of you –"

"Great Aunt Anne!" gasped Edward.

"She's coming out here!" squeaked Bridget.

Suddenly everything was happening in a great rush. Bridget pushed the onions and loaf into her egg basket, and then she gave Nat Cobbley a shove in his paunch so he fell backwards into a heap of old straw in the corner.

"Quick!" she snapped. "Cover him over!"

They were barely in time. Bits of Nat Cobbley were still showing quite plainly when the doorway darkened behind them.

Edward turned round hastily and made his bow. Great Aunt Anne was a dragon about manners. Actually, she was a dragon about more or less everything.

"What are you doing playing about with that straw?" she demanded. She was carrying a wooden spoon, and Edward realised with a sinking heart that he was probably in for his second beating of the day.

"Edward has been driving away a great rat, madam," said Bridget, with a curtsey. She'd always been a brilliant liar. "It was in the hen run, and then it dashed in here. It would have killed the hens for sure if Edward hadn't chased it away."

Of course Great Aunt Anne believed Bridget at once. Grown-ups always *did* believe Bridget. It was deeply unfair, because Great Aunt Anne never believed *Edward*, not even if he happened to be telling the truth.

"Well, you can both get back to work now," she said grudgingly. "Quick, it's nearly supper time!"

Bridget hurried out to the hen run, and Edward quickly gathered up a big bundle of firewood. Great Aunt Anne stood over him while he did it.

They left Nat Cobbley lying as still as a stone under the heap of dirty straw.

Chapter 3

Edward and Bridget slept downstairs on sacks of straw when Great Aunt Anne was visiting, and it seemed to Edward that he'd only just got himself comfortable when Bridget started poking him in the ribs.

"Go away," he muttered. But that just made her poke him even harder.

"Ouch!"

"Hush! Edward, are you awake?"

He opened an eye.

"How can I help but be awake when you keep poking me?" he asked.

Bridget ignored this.

"There's someone scratching at the shutters," she said. "It'll be that Cobbley man wanting his supper."

Edward yawned. Great Aunt Anne had made both the children do chores all evening, so they'd never got a chance to go back out to the barn.

"You'd better open the door before he wakes the whole house," went on Bridget. "I've left some food on the shelf behind the mugs."

Edward got up into the cool summer night. He lifted aside the beam that held the door closed and peered out into the darkness. Far away a dog barked briefly: there were lots of dogs in the town now, to warn their owners of thieving vagrants.

Yes, there was someone out there.

"Master Edward?" asked a low voice.

"Yes, I'm just getting your supper, Master Cobbley," whispered Edward.

The house was very quiet, and Edward was extremely careful as he lifted down the wooden mugs. He felt gently along the shelf. Yes, there was a loaf of bread, and there ... yes, there was a nearly full jug (filled with ale, by the smell of it), an onion, and a piece of cheese.

Edward very carefully put the mugs back on the shelf, very carefully picked up the jug and the food, and very carefully made his way back to the door.

Nat Cobbley was waiting there. Edward could just see the shape of his cap against the night sky.

Nat Cobbley stuffed the food down the front of his jerkin and took possession of the jug of ale.

"Good lad," he muttered. "You've done well. I shall make sure Sir Robert Cecil hears of this."

And then he turned, caught his foot on the chicken-food bucket, and fell headlong into a broom, two rakes, three flowerpots and a wheelbarrow.

The noise was enough to wake the dead. It certainly woke the fifteen dogs who lived in the street – and they, of course, woke everyone else.

Great Aunt Anne didn't help matters by jumping up from her bed and using a candlestick to bang the frying pan she took to bed with her in case of burglars.

The fact that she was shrieking *Murder! Murder! MURDER!* didn't help much, either.

Something whisked past Edward like the ghost of a frightened goose and began pulling Cobbley to his feet.

"Quick!" Bridget squawked, breathlessly. "Edward, help him!"

They got Cobbley to his feet. He must have hit his head, because he hardly seemed to know where he was.

"Quick," said Bridget again, kicking Cobbley's ale jug into a bush. "They're letting the dogs loose! We'll have to get him into the house!"

"But where on earth are we going to put him?" asked Edward, ducking his head under Cobbley's smelly armpit.

That was a good question. Cobbley was much too fat to fit in the chest or up the chimney.

"Under Great Aunt Anne's bed?" suggested Bridget, despairingly.

"But Great Aunt Anne's still in her room! How about ... how about in the **jakes**?"

"Don't be ridiculous!"

By the time they'd managed to steer Cobbley through the doorway there were sounds of movement upstairs.

"Father's coming down!" said Edward.

"Quick! Under the table with him!"

Father came running down the stairs carrying a stout stick and his dagger, and hurried out into the garden just in time to meet the first of his neighbours' dogs.

Everything got even more confused after that. Great Aunt Anne came down, too, and the

sight of her with all
of yesterday's white
make-up smudged
everywhere was
enough to send two
of the dogs howling
home with their
tails between
their legs.

"Well, there's no sign of anyone now," said Father, at last, when all the neighbours and the dogs had had a good nose around the garden and the stables and the barn. "He must have been trying to break into the house. Thank heavens he fell over the wheelbarrow and roused everyone."

Mistress Baker from next door shook her head.

"The constable is too old," she grumbled. "He could hardly catch a lame goat, let alone one of these vagrants that have got everywhere."

When at last everyone had gone home, and Great Aunt Anne had finished complaining about having to come and keep house for Father while Mother was away visiting (even though everyone had done their best to convince her there was no need), Edward and Bridget settled themselves down again on their sacks.

"I shall be so sleepy at school tomorrow that I'm bound to get whipped again," said Edward, sadly, pulling up his cover.

"Never mind, lad," said a hoarse voice from under the table. "Think of the service you are doing for the Queen!"

Bridget muttered something about the Queen that Edward hoped very much Nat Cobbley couldn't hear.

"And think of getting rid of that dog-hearted villain your schoolmaster, too," went on Nat Cobbley.

"This is crazed," hissed Bridget in her brother's ear. "You know that, don't you? Totally, totally crazed. That man is nothing but a fobbing jolt-head, and all he's going to bring us is trouble."

Edward sighed. Nat Cobbley had brought him more than enough trouble already. Still, it'd all be well worth it if they could get rid of Master Thatcham.

If they could.

Nat Cobbley had begun munching his onion, but Edward settled his cheek down against the rough sacking and, very worried and confused, tried to get to sleep.

Chapter 4

Edward ran straight home after school the next day, not even hanging around for a game of street football. He found Bridget in the kitchen, rubbing salt into a cheese.

"Where is he?" asked Edward.

Bridget jerked her head towards the barn.

"I gave him some bread and ale at noon, and the swag-bellied rogue had the cheek to moan that there was no pie," she snapped.

Edward looked around apprehensively.

"Where's Great Aunt Anne?"

"At her prayers."

Edward relaxed a little. Great Aunt Anne was very religious and prayed in her room for at least an hour before supper. You could sometimes hear the snores of holiness right down in the kitchen.

"Master Thatcham whipped Will Hobson today, just because Will had a cough," Edward told his sister. "You know, Master Thatcham does have a desperate look about him, Bridget."

"I'm not surprised, being locked up with you lot all day."

"But Bridget, if Master Thatcham really is a traitor –"

Bridget rounded on him.

"Well, what if he is?" she demanded. "All that flap-mouthed Cobbley's done is lie around stinking, and stuffing his fat guts. The Queen's spy? He can't even walk down the garden path without rousing half the street! When's he going to *do* something?"

"Well, how should I know?" grumbled Edward.

"It would help if you asked him," she snapped. "But there, I have to do everything, don't I?"

Bridget flounced out, wiping her hands on her apron as she went.

Great Aunt Anne wasn't the only one sleeping the evening away, but Bridget was merciless. She prodded Nat Cobbley with her foot until he suddenly sat up and shouted, "No, no! It wasn't me, your worship!"

Bridget didn't allow him any time to gather his wits.

"When are you going to start spying on Master Thatcham?" she demanded.

Cobbley pulled a filthy rag out of his sleeve and used it to wipe his face.

"Well, Mistress Bridget," he said. "I must gather information from round the town, first."

"What sort of information?"

Cobbley waved a vague hand.

"Where he lives, who his friends are ..."

Bridget nodded.

"That's easily done," she said briskly. "He has a house at the back of the school, and no friends at all. Everybody hates him. You'd best break into his house tonight and see what you can find out."

Then she turned to Edward.

"And you can go with him, Edward, to make sure he doesn't get lost on the way."

"But –" said Cobbley.

"But –" said Edward.

But Bridget was already walking back to the kitchen, her skirts bouncing angrily around her as she went.

That night Bridget pushed Edward out into the garden while he was still more than half asleep.

"I'll leave the door on the latch," she whispered. "Just don't make a racket coming back from the schoolhouse and wake up the neighbours again."

Cobbley was waiting inside the barn.

"This might be dangerous, lad," he said, uneasily, as they slipped out through the garden gate. "Perhaps you should stay here. I can tell you what happens."

"It's no good, Master Cobbley," sighed Edward. "Bridget will have you arrested by the constable unless I can swear to her that you really went."

"But surely a sweet little thing like your sister wouldn't ..."

"You don't know Bridget," said Edward, gloomily.

It was quite dark in the streets, but the lights shining through the little diamond-shaped panes of the Guild Hall lit up the school opposite.

"The aldermen are having a meeting," Edward explained. "Father's there."

He led the way round to where the schoolmaster's little house leaned drunkenly against the back of the main building. Edward swallowed hard. It'd been easy enough to think *we'll spy on Master Thatcham*, but faced with this dark house, and knowing that the schoolmaster was so very close ...

"Perhaps we should wait a bit longer, to make sure he's asleep," suggested Edward.

"He'll have risen at five this morning to get to class," said Cobbley. "He'll be sound asleep sure enough."

Edward could hardly imagine the punishment you'd get for breaking into Master Thatcham's house. It was bad enough if you hadn't learned your homework ...

Edward gasped. He'd run home that afternoon in such a hurry he'd left his homework book behind in the schoolroom. He usually learned his homework at breakfast time, but if he'd forgotten his book ...

He gulped. Whatever happened now, he was doomed. Completely doomed.

Cobbley had drawn his dagger, and in a moment the door to Master Thatcham's house was opening silently in front of them. Cobbley stepped over the threshold and Edward followed close behind him. The windows were shuttered, and only the faintest chinks of blue or silver light came in round the edges.

The first thing that hit Edward was the smell. Living in a town meant he was used to all sorts of stinks, but this ...

Cobbley sniffed.

"By my beard, I never came across a schoolmaster who wore rose-petal perfume before," he muttered.

"He usually just stinks of cider," said Edward, in great surprise.

They moved forward cautiously.

The room in which they found themselves was almost empty, but there was a staircase on the right and a door to the left.

"Master Cobbley," said Edward, in the smallest possible whisper. "I've forgotten my Latin book."

Cobbley snorted quietly.

"If the schoolmaster finds us here, I doubt he'll be wanting us to recite any verse to him."

"But that door leads to the schoolroom where I've left my book and I need it to get my homework done for tomorrow," whispered Edward. "Look, I won't be long."

The door opened, as
he'd known it would,
into a room filled with
benches, moonlight,
and the scent of
misery. Edward went
quickly over to the
cloak hooks, found
his book, and shoved
it down the back of
his **doublet** for safe
keeping.

Then, feeling oddly
stronger, he went back
to Cobbley, who was
waiting for him at the
bottom of the stairs.

Cobbley bent down
to whisper ticklishly in
Edward's ear.

"Keep to the sides of
the stairs, boy, so they
don't creak."

Edward did keep to the sides of the stairs, but they still creaked. Each time they did, Cobbley froze for ages before moving on.

All too soon the stairs came to an end. The windows up here weren't shuttered, and the moon shone in mistily through the **oiled linen windows**. They'd come up into a room open to the rafters.

There was a bed draped round with curtains in front of them, and a door to their right. Cobbley put his ear to it.

"Can you hear anything?" whispered Edward.

"No. But I can smell all sorts. That's the jakes."

"So ... that must be his bed, then!" breathed Edward.

In the misty moonlight the curtains were the colour of a dead man's blood.

Cobbley hesitated.

"Perhaps we'd do better to come back another time," he whispered. "Perhaps on Monday when he's at school. Yes, that would be best."

Edward quite honestly agreed with him, but then he thought about Bridget and traitors and he clenched his fists to give himself courage.

"Bridget will report you unless we do something tonight," he whispered. "And anyway, his plot against the Queen might be planned for tomorrow!"

Nat Cobbley sighed, and settled his grip on his dagger.

"Very well, if we must," he said.

The moonlight had laid a silver sheen on the table by the window. It was covered with pieces of paper.

They tiptoed to the table and began to search, Edward all the time aware that Master Thatcham was just behind those bed hangings behind him.

There wasn't much light but now that Edward looked closely at the pieces of paper, they didn't look much like letters. They looked more like ...

... *recipes?*

Cobbley had turned his attention to the chest by the wall. He'd just put his fingers carefully under the lid when –

"Thieves!" screamed a voice behind them.

Edward's heart jolted so violently it nearly knocked his teeth out.

"Help! *Help!*" screamed a voice from behind the bed curtains. "Husband – save me! Thieves! **Cut-purses! Vagabonds!**"

Edward gaped. But that was a *woman's* voice! And ... *husband?*

Cobbley acted while Edward was still

frozen with bewilderment
and terror.

"Quick!" he shouted.
He rushed over,
grabbed Edward's
arm and pushed him
towards the stairs.
"Run for your life,
boy. RUN!"

Chapter 5

Edward ended up falling down most of the stairs. He whacked his elbow and his knee hard, but he was too busy being terrified to worry about whether he'd hurt himself or not.

He ended up, dizzy and panicking, sprawled across the stone flags. Something huge was crashing down the stairs after him and he had a horrible feeling it was Nat Cobbley. Above Edward's head the woman was still screaming fit to wake the whole town.

(Woman? *Woman??*)

Edward pushed himself to his feet. They had to get out of the house fast. He ran two steps, tripped over a stool, and ended up crashing into a wall. Edward crawled along the wall, feverishly feeling his way.

Someone was coming down the stairs.

"A light! Bring a light!" someone shouted, terrifyingly close.

Master Thatcham! That was Master Thatcham's voice!

Edward crawled even faster. If he could only find the ...

"Aargh!" he gasped, hitting his head on something which, horribly, said *Aargh!* too.

"Master Edward?" came a hoarse whisper.

"Master Cobbley?"

"I've lost my dagger," Cobbley hissed. "When I fell down the —" but whatever else he was going to say was drowned out by a tremendous banging outside.

"Open! Ho, there! What's amiss?"

"There's the constable!" squeaked Edward. "He must have heard all the screaming!"

"Quick, lad!" whispered Cobbley. "Here's the door!"

Edward grabbed Cobbley's sleeve and let himself be pulled through the door ...

... straight into the glinting, moonlit schoolroom.

Edward stared around in horror. They must have got so dizzy tumbling down the stairs that they'd come through the wrong door!

A new hammering came from the street side of the room.

Edward turned to go back – and stopped.

There was a shadowy figure in the schoolhouse doorway, lit by the flickering candle it held in its hand.

Master Thatcham.

Edward, filled with terror, recoiled, fell over a bench, and sat down hard.

Master Thatcham took a step into the room, a thin smile on his lips.

"A thief, eh?" he said, his face as intent as a snake's. "Well, that's the constable at the door, you villain, and you'll soon be hanging in the market square."

It was then that Edward realised that Master Thatcham hadn't seen him. In the confusion of the darkness he'd gone unnoticed.

Cobbley let out a laugh. It sounded as merry as a baby's funeral.

"You turn me over to the constable, master, and I'll tell everyone your little secret," he said. "A sober unmarried man – isn't that what the schoolmaster in this place has to be? And all the time you're a cider-sipping villain who keeps a wife hidden away in his bedroom!"

Master Thatcham laughed scornfully.

"There's no one in this whole town who will listen to you," he said. "Believe a filthy vagrant? They'll stretch your neck for you first!"

Edward could hardly breathe from terror, but somehow, without ever deciding to, he found himself getting to his feet.

He meant to be silent, but a bench scraped on the stone floor and Master Thatcham gave a great start and peered past the candle flame.

"Who's that? *Edward Glover?*"

Edward swallowed hard.

"They'll believe *me!*" he said.

Master Thatcham stood staring for a moment, the candlelight turning his face into a thing of hollows and ridges, like a death mask. Then he turned swiftly to the master's desk. Edward thought he'd gone for the **birch**, but when Master Thatcham turned round he was holding something which gleamed in the candlelight.

His penknife. That was Master Thatcham's penknife. But –

"Run!" bellowed Cobbley. "Run, you little fool, or he'll gut you like a fish. Run!"

Edward ran. He scrambled wildly over the rows of benches – but the street door would be locked, so there was no escape that way. Where could he go?

Upwards. Only upwards. Edward threw himself at the row of cloak hooks and managed to pull himself up to reach the rafters that held up the roof.

Edward got his knee safely on the first rafter and looked down. Master Thatcham was advancing on Cobbley, his knife held out threateningly in front of him.

"No one will blame me if a thief gets killed," Master Thatcham said nastily. "Or if his accomplice falls to his death."

"Edward, get out of here," said Cobbley.

"But –"

"I'll deal with this. Just go!"

The rafters made a maze through the darkness under the thatch of the roof, but Edward could see one small star. That would be where there was a hole in the roof to let out the smoke of the fire. The old schoolroom hadn't had a modern chimney installed yet.

It wasn't an easy climb: there was one nasty moment when Edward's foot slipped, and another when a bat came and flew dizzyingly around

his head, but gradually he made his way closer
and closer to that single shining star. At last he
pushed himself through the hole in the roof and
took a deep breath of the night air.

The aldermen's feast must have come to an end, for the street was filled with servants bearing torches, and men in long fur-edged gowns.

Edward filled his lungs.

"He's trying to kill him!" he shouted as loud as he could. "Master Thatcham's got a wife! He's trying to kill him and he's got a wife!"

A dozen faces turned up towards him.

"Edward?" said someone. That was Father's voice.

"Yes, Father, it's me!" Edward called, leaning out to try to see him. "It's me, Father! Help! Master Thatcham's trying to kill us!"

But then he must have leaned too far, or else the old thatch of the roof gave way, because somehow he was falling forwards and sliding down the thatch towards the cliff-edge drop to the street below.

Just before the edge, a button on his doublet got snagged on the thatch and dragged him to a stop. Edward lay, his eyes squeezed tight, hardly daring to breathe. If he moved a muscle the button might come off and then ...

Below him all the men were shouting.

There was an awful pause, and then from the top of the roof a small eruption.

"Lad?" gasped a hoarse voice. "It's all right, I'll soon get you. You just stay where you are!"

Edward felt something touch his left hand. He opened one eye and made out the end of Nat Cobbley's leather belt.

"Grab it, boy. Grab it!"

Edward moved his hand a fraction, but even this movement was enough to send him slithering further down the thatch, and only a violent squirm and a fierce clutch at the belt allowed him to get hold of it.

He got both hands to the belt and lay face down, his legs hanging into space and his heart hammering.

"Right, then," said Cobbley, gruffly. "You hold on tight, young Edward, and I can pull you back up. Then we'll soon have you down to ground again, safe and sound."

It took rather a long time to explain everything.

"A *wife?*" said Alderman Coote, astonished. "The schoolmaster has a *wife?* But under the terms of his job ..."

Cobbley smiled grimly at Master Thatcham, whom he'd trussed up in the schoolmaster's gown.

"You'd best be packing," he said, with satisfaction.

Edward tried to look as stern as the aldermen, but he just couldn't stop a great grin spreading all over his face. All evening he'd been feeling less and less sure about whether Master Thatcham really was part of a plot against the Queen. But thanks to Nat Cobbley, Master Thatcham had got the sack, and that was so wonderful Edward found he didn't really care about anything else.

"Hmm," said the old constable. "Talking of packing, Cobbley, what's your job? Because if ever I've seen a filthy vagrant in need of whipping ..."

There was a nasty pause.

Edward tugged his father's sleeve.

"If you please, sir," he said. "Nat Cobbley is ever so brave and strong, isn't he? I'm sure he'd be useful about the house and garden."

Edward's father looked doubtful.

"Well," he said, "I was thinking perhaps a reward ..."

"It'll be all right," said Edward. "Really, sir. Bridget'll keep him from being any trouble. He saved my life after all!"

And at that Edward's father sighed, and told the constable that the man Cobbley seemed to be one of his servants.

Nat Cobbley wasn't as pleased about his new job as Edward would have thought.

"But what a come-down," he said. "From Sir Robert Cecil's spy to this – servitude." He sighed. "There, but beggars can't be choosers, I suppose."

And, touching his filthy hand to his filthy head in salute to his new master, he followed Edward and his father glumly home.

Glossary

aldermen members of an English town council, next in importance to the mayor

ale a weak alcoholic drink

birch bundle of birch branches for whipping people

cut-purses thieves

doublet close-fitting jacket for men and boys

(hang) **draw and quarter** punishment for treason, the traitor being hanged then his body chopped into four pieces

hose tight leggings, often striped, worn by men

jakes toilet

jerkin sleeveless jacket

minstrels travelling musicians and singers

oiled linen windows windows made of oil-soaked cloth rather than glass

quill pen made from a large feather

vagabond criminal with no settled home

vagrant person with no settled home or regular work